This book belongs to

Made in the USA
Coppell, TX
03 May 2021

54961044R10069